MARRIAGE
LICENSE
HANDBOOK

Judith A. Kaluzny, JD

Publisher's Cataloging-In-Publication Data
(Prepared by The Donohue Group, Inc.)
Names: Kaluzny, Judith A., author.
Title: Marriage license handbook / Judith A. Kaluzny, JD.
Description: [Fullerton, California] : Judith A. Kaluzny, [2022]
Identifiers: ISBN 9798985688603 (paperback) | ISBN 9798985688610 (ebook)
Subjects: LCSH: Marriage law--California--Handbooks, manuals, etc. |
Married people--California--Finance, Personal--Handbooks, manuals, etc.
| Unmarried couples--California--Finance, Personal--Handbooks, manuals,
etc. | LCGFT: Handbooks and manuals.
Classification: LCC KFC120 .K35 2022 (print) | LCC KFC120 (ebook) | DDC
346.794016--dc23

*Every person who falsely personates another,
and in such assumed character marries or
pretends to marry, or to sustain the
marriage relation towards another,
with or without the connivance
of such other, is guilty of a felony.*

PC §528 1872

*To be ignorant of one's ignorance is
the malady of the ignorant.*

Amos Alcott
American teacher/writer/
philosopher/reformer

Contents

Part 1:
Introduction

A Unique License

When I had to renew my California driver's license, I studied a little booklet, California Driver Handbook and read sample tests so I could ace the 18-questions on the official written examination. I also had to pass an eye test; I did not need to take the road test this time.

My basic driver's license allows me to operate a single motor vehicle anywhere in the state.

If I wanted to operate a vehicle that transports sixteen or more passengers, a motorcycle, or a commercial vehicle, I would have had to study for and take a different written test and road test. The first time I applied for a driver's license, I would have had to include proof of my identity, proof of my Social Security number, and proof of my California address with my application.

When Michael Pollan, a journalism professor at Berkeley, wanted to prepare a 100 percent natural meal so he could include the experience in his book *The Omnivore's Dilemma: A Natural History of Four Meals*, he first had to secure a hunting license. That meant determining which of the seven types of licenses to obtain, taking a fourteen-hour class, and passing a 100-question test. His hunting license allowed him to kill a wild animal, which he could then skin, cook, eat–and record for posterity in his 2007 Penguin Books title.

Remarkably, he did not need a license to buy a high-powered rifle. To buy any gun, one must have a firearm safety certificate issued by the California Department of Justice, Bureau of Firearms—which requires passing a 30-question written test based on a 50-page instruction booklet. And one must pass a background check. As the *California Carry* website says, "Do you like jumping through flaming hoops? Then buying a gun in California is just the process for you!"

> *It took me a couple of months to sort out the procedures for securing a hunter's license, which involved enrolling in a hunter education course and taking a test. It seems they'll sell a high-powered rifle to just about anybody in California, but it's against the law to aim the thing at an animal without first enduring a fourteen-hour class and a one-hundred-question multiple choice exam that demands some study. The next scheduled session was on a Saturday two months off.*

Michael Pollan
The Omnivore's Dilemma, The Penguin Press 2007

Contrast that with securing a license to share your wealth, your earnings, your home with another person, to take on the risk of crushing debt you didn't bargain for, to have property that you own only half of, property that someone else can control, to take on the possibility of creating life, to face the possibility of a ruinous divorce one day down the line. To share a bed and take on the emotional baggage of another person. A license to marry entitles you to all that—and possible endless bliss.

But to obtain a marriage license, one only has to complete a 9-question application that asks: What is your name? Birth name? Address? Date of birth? State of birth? Previous marriage? If yes, ended how and when? Your father's name and birthplace? Your mother's name and birthplace?

Did you ace this quiz? Of course you did–which means the clerk, as Deputy Commissioner of Civil Marriage, could marry you on the spot provided you can pay the license fee that varies from county to county. Your Marriage License will allow you to:

- Change your name*
- Share your wealth, your earnings, and your home with another person
- Have or buy property you only own half of that someone else can control
- Take on the risk of someone else's crushing debt
- Take on the financial responsibility and emotional baggage of your spouse as well as their current and any co-created future children
- Face the possibility of ruinous divorce someday down the line

All that–with no test to pass or handbook to study. Does that make a lot of sense to you? As the founder of The Safe and Sane Divorce Project and a divorce lawyer and mediator for over forty years, it does not make any sense to me.

* If you choose to change names, the clerk will give you a page of information including links to genetic diseases, HIV/AIDS, and domestic violence.

What you don't know...

Marriage is a life-changing event, the prelude to hopefully…supposedly…possibly long-term partnership. Although its license is actually a legally binding contract, "Its provisions are unwritten, its penalties are unspecified, and the terms of the contract are typically unknown to the 'contracting parties.'" Yet the State provides no handbook, no fact sheet, not even a list of things to consider about how entering into a marriage will affect your legal and financial rights and obligations. In fact, when I volunteered for Law Day activities as a student, I learned that my local school district did not allow attorneys in the program to discuss family law with high-school seniors at all because "it would promote divorce."

That's the good old ignorance-is-bliss school of thought, and although things have changed a great deal since those "what you don't know can't hurt you" times, most people still enter into a marriage with both eyes closed, expecting eternal bliss will somehow simply work out.

"Prospective spouses are neither informed of the terms of the contract nor are they allowed any options about these terms. In fact, one wonders how many men and women would agree to the marriage contract if they were given the opportunity to read it and to consider their rights and obligations to which they were committing themselves."

Legal Regulation of Marriage: Tradition and Change
62 California Law Review
1169 at 1170.

Terms and Limitations

The California Family Code[1] has 9,340 items of statutory law, definitions, and policy regarding marriage, partnership, divorce, children, adoption, and surrogacy; 15 rules about the Family Law Facilitator; 804 rules about the Department of Child Support Services; and 43 codes regarding pilot programs. No one has ever counted the number of family law cases in which the codes and rules have been interpreted by the various courts of appeal and Supreme Court of California..

This Book is Not Legal Advice

The limited information in this handbook applies specifically to California, a community property state. It may be applicable to some extent in other community property states, but their laws vary in the details. As of 2021, only nine are community property states: Arizona, California, Idaho, Louisiana, Nevada, New Mexico, Texas, Washington, and Wisconsin. You can have community property in Alaska if the married couple agrees in writing that their property shall be community. The rest of

---

[1] Reference is made to the Family Code of the State of California. "Codes" are the laws of the state, such as Civil Code, Health and Welfare Code, Penal Code and Probate Code. Reference is made to specific laws in the Family Code, known as sections of the code, by "Fam.C. § 000."

the country uses "common law" or an "equitable distribution" division of marital property, which can be what a judge thinks is fair, not necessarily equal.

Some of the rules in this handbook might seem contradictory. One law, for example, states all property acquired during marriage is community, while another code states you can acquire separate property during marriage. The devil is in the details.

This handbook of minimal education and questions is intended to help you understand what you and your prospective spouse are getting into so you will have fewer unpleasant surprises that might cause lasting hostility or suspicion or resentments between you. And, just possibly, the extra knowledge will help you have more trust and open communication from the beginning of your wedded bliss—which might, in turn, help you stay together after the stars have left your eyes and urgency-to-wed has been replaced by the realities of sharing all that daily life as a couple has to offer.

Marriage Defined

Marriage is a personal relation arising from a civil contract between two persons, to which the consent of the parties capable of making that contract is necessary. Consent alone does not constitute marriage. Consent must be followed by the issuance of a license and solemnization, more commonly known as a ceremony.

After marriage, wife and husband are each other's "spouse."

The License

A marriage license is a public document issued by the county clerk. Due to COVID-19 protocols, you must now complete your marriage license application online. That means you must also be able to upload a current valid identification card, proof of divorce if you divorced within the previous three months, and proof of death if your previous spouse died while you were married.

You do not need a blood test to get married in California. You don't even need to prove citizenship or live in the state. But you must have a computer, laptop, tablet, or smartphone with audio and visual capability to book a virtual marriage ceremony, and both parties must be in the same room in the State of California at both the time you apply for the marriage license and when the virtual marriage ceremony is performed. Most counties offer a virtual marriage license & ceremony package. Fees and ceremony availability vary from county to county.

You can find information about your county at California State Association of Counties <counties.org/county-websites-profile-information> or searching for "county clerk office near me."

Marriageable Age

Both parties must be over the age of eighteen to marry unless they have the consent of one parent and a judge. If the minor has no parent, a court may grant permission to the minor. The judge must ensure the minor is informed about:

1. The rights and responsibilities of an emancipated minor, including:

    - How to leave home, stay in a shelter, and separate from parents or guardian

    - Whether consent of the parent or guardian is needed to stay away

    - Rights to apply for restraining orders

    - Rights to sign contracts for legal services and mental health counseling

2. Why and how to get the marriage canceled by a court

3. The procedures for legal separation or dissolution of marriage

4. Telephone numbers for the National Domestic Violence Hotline and the National Sexual Assault Hotline

The judge might also require premarital counseling about the "social, economic, and personal responsibilities incident to marriage." Incredibly, this vital counseling is not required for anyone, whether under or over eighteen.

It seems to me unlikely in these times that teenagers would plead with parents for consent to marry. Wouldn't they just cohabit? Used to be kids married because of pregnancy so the child would not be "illegitimate." In 1970 in California 12.6% of all children born were to unmarried parents. In 2018, it was 35.7%. In 1973 the concept of illegitimacy was abolished in all states, see below.

How to get married

1. Consent is essential

Who is capable of consenting? Anyone over age 18 "...and not otherwise disqualified, are capable of consenting to and consummating marriage" (Fam. C. §301). A marriage could be set aside–annulled–if a person's consent was forced or obtained by trickery (fraud) or if the person did not have capacity to freely and knowingly consent.

A person could have the marriage annulled by a court if her or his consent was fraudulently obtained consent.

A marriage might be annulled if a person lied about something so serious the other person would not have married if they knew the true facts. For instance, a man did not tell his fiancée he'd already had a vasectomy when the couple talked about having children. Or a citizen of another country secretly just wants to stay in the United States.

I did an annulment of my second marriage after just a few weeks. I think it helped with the judge that I was a local lawyer, because I listened as the court denied two other women who applied for annulments in later-life marriages–and I thought their cases were better than mine!

2. Choose Your Names

Choose the names you will use as a married person. The Name Equality Act went into effect January 1, 2009 (Fam. C. §306.5). You can change your middle and last name by means of the marriage-license application. You may use the current last name of either spouse. You may use the last name of either of you as given at birth. You may combine your current or birth names totally or a part of each. Smith and Moore could become Smoore. Or you can use both last names with a hyphen in between.

3. Obtain the License

Apply for a marriage license online at your local county clerk office. You can find information about your county at California State Association of Counties <counties.org/county-websites-profile-information> or searching for "county clerk office near me."

The license is good for 90 days; it then expires. There are no refunds. Errors cannot be corrected, so be careful how you list the married names you decide on.

4. Solemnize the Marriage

A solemnizer is the person who "performs" the marriage ceremony. You can use the county clerk in a virtual marriage ceremony.

If you choose your own solemnizer, give them your license before the ceremony. If they think the stated facts are correct, you can proceed to tie the knot. After you have each stated that you consent to the marriage, the solemnizer states that you are now married. No particular words are required.

Choose Your Solemnizer

The county clerk is designated as a commissioner of civil marriages, so she or he can perform your marriage. Captains of the Salvation Army may perform a marriage. A shaman or medicine man or woman, if recognized by the tribe as the religious leader, can perform a marriage. Your congressman or your assemblyman or senator can perform your marriage. A sitting or retired judge, a sitting or retired court commissioner, a justice or retired justice of the Supreme Court of the United States can all perform marriages.

Choose a Personal Solemnizer

In some California counties, the county clerk can deputize someone of your choice to be the solemnizer. The deputization lasts one day, and the person does not have to be a California resident.

Alternative Solemnizer

If you belong to a religious society or denomination that has no clergy to perform marriages, Fam. C. §307 allows for an alternative choice that essentially lets you use anyone registered to solemnize marriages as long as the license is properly completed and filed with the county recorder within 10 days.

5. The Consent

In any words you like, you both declare "in the presence of the person solemnizing the marriage and necessary witnesses, that they take each other as husband and wife." (Fam. C. §425.)

That simple statement, usually enacted by each party saying, "I do" to some form of the question, "Do you take this person to be your lawfully wedded husband/

wife, etc.," is hardly informed consent, is it? No one ever asks, "Do you accept the financial consequences of this marriage contract?"

Thinking back, I realize I did not have free consent when I got married. I don't remember being at the altar or saying anything that day, much less, "I do."

I was 20 years old, depressed, and essentially coerced by Mother, because as a female I didn't count unless I was married.

6. Finish and File the License

The solemnizer dates the license and adds the city and county of the marriage and the names and residences of the witnesses. You need at least one but no more than two witnesses who are able to sign their names and understand what is going on. The solemnizer's official position, name, and address must be typed in or printed on the license. Finally, the solemnizer must return the completed marriage license to the county clerk's office within 10 days.

To get a copy of your marriage certificate, you have to pay a fee. If you lose your marriage license or there's no record of it having been recorded, you or your spouse can purchase a certificate from the county clerk. That, too, is now done online.

7. Health Coverage (Recommended)

You and your spouse can apply for joint health insurance if you file within 60 days of your marriage, whether you buy private insurance or use Covered California. This is not a requirement, but it is highly recommended.

In pre-COVID times, you would be given The State Department of Health Services brochure *Your Future Together, Health Information You Need To Know*, which contains information about genetics, AIDS, and domestic violence. Nothing required either or each of you to read it. It is just one page, available online, and contains:

1. A note about the Name Equality Act of 2007
2. Advice for living a healthy lifestyle
3. Information about genetic defects and diseases and a list of centers that test for and treat genetic defects and diseases

4. Information about acquired immune deficiency syndrome (AIDS) and where to get tested and/or treated for antibodies to AIDS' probable causative agent
5. Information about domestic violence, including resources available to victims and a statement that physical, emotional, psychological, and sexual abuse, as well as assault and battery, are against the law

It does not contain information about your future financial rights and responsibilities as married people.

Confidential Marriage

When two people who have been living together as spouses (husband and wife, husband and husband, or wife and wife) want to make their marriage legal without letting anyone, especially their children, know they haven't been married all along, they can ask for a "confidential marriage." Confidential marriage licenses cost more than ordinary licenses, but they do not require a witness and their records are not available as public documents. The confidential marriage records can be obtained only by court order or by one of the spouses.

Registered Domestic Partnership

Domestic partners are two adults who have chosen to share one another's lives in an intimate and committed relationship of mutual caring. A popular status in California before same-sex marriage was recognized as legal, domestic partnerships are established by filing a Declaration of Domestic Partnership with the Secretary of State. All of the following requirements must be met:

1. Neither person is married to someone else or is a member of another domestic partnership with someone else that has not been terminated, dissolved, or adjudged a nullity.

2. The two persons are not related by blood in a way that would prevent them from being married to each other in this state.

3. Both persons are at least 18 years of age. The permissions required for marriage under the age of 18 apply for domestic partnerships as well.

4. Both persons are capable of consenting to the domestic partnership.

   - Registered domestic partners have the same rights, protections, and benefits, and are subject to the same responsibilities, obligations, and duties under law, whether they derive from statutes, administrative regulations, court rules, government policies, common law, or any other provisions or sources of law, as are granted to and imposed upon spouses.

The key differences between a domestic partnership and a marriage involve the rights provided. Married couples can transfer assets to one another without paying gift taxes or estate taxes. Domestic partners cannot.

Domestic partnerships are not recognized by the Federal government, including the Social Security administration. You cannot apply for social security disability on your partner's behalf or collect survivor benefits if your partner dies.

Some insurance policies do not recognize domestic partners as married spouses. This can mean limits on insurance coverage and increased out-of-pocket expenses for medical or dental treatment if your partner does not have their own insurance.

Domestic partners must file their taxes separately rather than jointly. This means you may face issues with deductions and various tax savings married couples would qualify for.

Your partner can adopt your child from a separate marriage or partnership, but the other biological parent must relinquish their parental rights.

I attended a christening party for a baby adopted by two men in a partnership–who could not get legally married until years later. I then mediated a pre-nup agreement for them, noting how typical of modern life: first you have the baby, then you get married!

Part 2:
The Contract

The Marriage Contract

The contract between spouses is based on "obligations of mutual respect, fidelity, and support" (Fam. C. §720).

In other words, your "I do" means that, by law, you promise to deal with your spouse with "highest good faith and fair dealing."

It also means all the profits of your work from that point now belong to the two of you equally, even if you keep separate bank accounts. Community property essentially means "What's mine is yours and what's yours is mine." You may think your pillow-talk agreement to split the housework and bills is legally binding, but not in California.

Unless you have a prenuptial agreement. Or unless you write and sign post-nuptial agreements.

You are now in a new "confidential" and "fiduciary" relationship in which "Neither shall take any unfair advantage of the other." And while that sounds right and reasonable in those first, starry-eyed hours, days, or weeks of marriage, National Public Radio (NPR) reported that 87% of people will eventually lie to their spouses about money.

And those lies–those breaches of fiduciary obligation to your spouse–have legal consequences, and your spouse can demand you pay that money back to the community pot.

A woman initiated divorce after her 12-year-old daughter discovered her father's infidelity online. His affair had been going on for five years. Wife was outraged at the money he'd spent on the other woman while she pinched household expenses.

A public official who did not want his dirty laundry aired in court, he readily agreed in mediation to account for every penny. He assembled a two-inch-thick packet documenting $40,000 spent on the affair. Upon sale of the community residence, he paid his wife $20,000 from his half of the proceeds.

Fiduciary Obligation

What kind of spending breaches your fiduciary obligation? Money squandered on gambling. Extramarital affairs. Even lavish gifts to your mother that your spouse did not agree to. A woman who did not reveal she had won the lottery ended up having to give all her winnings–not just half–when her ex-husband found out about the prize and took her to court.

Access Records

As part of the mutual fiduciary obligation, you are entitled to access, inspect, and copy any books your spouse keeps for any transaction or business–and, on request, you must, in turn, give your spouse true and full information about transaction you've made that affects or concerns any community property. You each hold any benefit or profit as a trustee for the other.

Management and Control

You both are entitled to "management and control" of marital (community) property, real and personal, Fam. C. 1100-1103. Personal property such as leases, automobiles, businesses, insurance, retirement accounts, bank accounts, dogs, furniture, boats – anything you own that is not real property. Real property includes land and buildings on the land.

But that does not mean you can do whatever you want with your little construction business, plumbing shop, accounting firm, Etsy store, or coaching practice without your spouse's knowledge and consent. Even if you have primary management and control of your community property business, you must still give your spouse advance written notice of any sale, lease, exchange, lien, or other disposition of all or substantially all the personal property used in the business.

Even if the business is in your sole name.

Even if it is a farm where the land is owned by someone else.

Even if you are a sharecropper.

Don't forget—you're married now.

When I was in law school, it seemed strange to me that women did not have any control over community property until 1975. Before then, the law said the rights in marriage to property were equal, but the husband had management and control of that property.

How could the rights to property be called "equal" when only one of the two allegedly equal parties can make decisions about that property?

Duty to Support

Your marriage contract also includes the mutual duty to support. If there is no community property, such as earnings, you must support your spouse from your separate property so long as you are living together. Support for a separated spouse could be by written agreement or by court order.

Community Property and Exceptions

In California, the default rule is that all real or personal property acquired during your marriage from your work or efforts is community. You and your spouse may hold title to real estate as joint tenants, as tenants in common, or as community property.

> *Joint Tenancy:* if one person dies, the surviving joint tenant(s) own the property; you cannot gift, sell, or will your share to anyone else.
>
> *Tenants in Common:* you can gift, sell, or will your share of property to someone else. If you do not include a restriction on residency and your tenant-in-common partner sells their share, you could find yourself forced to accept a stranger into your house.

You acquire property by means of your efforts, your work, your time. If you spend time online buying and selling stocks in a portfolio you owned before marriage, that account acquires some community interest. If you spend time and money fixing up a 1965 Mustang, it acquires some community value.

On a panel about how to improve family law, a judge said he would ban all references to community property and divorce law on television and in the movies.

In a lovely film with George Clooney as a popular womanizer and Catherine Zeta Jones as the woman who intends to take him down, she says to him the morning after their wedding: "Now I own half of everything you have," implying that sleeping together cinched the deal.

Wrong! Everything is still his.

I am surprised at how many educated people do not understand this.

Examples of Community Property

- Pensions
- 401(k)s
- IRAs
- Deferred compensation
- Stock options
- Bonuses
- Commissions
- Businesses
- Country Club memberships
- Annuities
- Life insurance
- Brokerage accounts (mutual funds, stocks, etc.)
- Bank accounts (checking, savings, Christmas Club, CDs, etc.)
- Professional practices and licenses
- Limited partnerships
- Vehicles (cars, boats, trucks, RVs, etc.)
- Art
- Antiques
- Tax refunds
- Earned income
- Inherited income deposited into a joint account

A client of mine had a thriving business for 11 years which she had established during her marriage. She wanted it to be her separate property, but the lawyer she consulted told her it had to be community property.

Bad advice. She and Husband could have written an agreement to keep the business her own separate property.

Separate property

All property you owned before marriage, all property you received during marriage by gift or inheritance and kept in your name alone, and proceeds and profits from that property is separate property. The Rolex watch you gave your spouse as a birthday gift is their separate property, as is the diamond tennis bracelet your spouse gave you on your birthday.

But if the two of you decide to buy gold jewelry for one of you as an investment in the value of gold, that jewelry is community property. Still, you can acquire separate property during marriage, despite the community-property presumption, if:

- You inherit property and keep the title in your name

- You inherit money and keep it in a separate account *Warning:* if you then use that money for a down payment on a house, keep good records as to where it came from because you can get it back later if you break up, although the refund will be without interest

- You receive a gift of money from your spouse or anyone else and keep it in a separate account *Warning:* if you claim your house is your property because your parents gifted you the down payment, you will have a hard time proving they really intended their son-in-law or daughter-in-law–the father or mother of their only grandchildren–to have no interest in his or her home.

- You are a trust-fund baby and make the down payment and all other payments on the house from those funds.

- You established specific types of future acquisitions or earnings as separate property in a written pre-nuptial or post-nuptial agreement. It is best to file it with the country recorder to put any creditors on official notice that community property and your spouse's earnings are not available to pay separate debts.

Property Transmutation

You can mutually agree in writing to change property from separate to community. This written agreement is called transmutation, and, as with any other marital contract, must be:

- Written to include the exact, specific terms and effects of the transmutation

- Signed and dated by the person who owns the separate property

- Filed with the county recorder if the transmutation is for real property

Transmutation can take place while you are not thinking of it. If you own an apartment building before marriage, for example, it is your separate property. If you have a management company take care of it, it stays separate. But if you are the one doing the repairs, interviewing tenants, and handling leases and evictions, the property's profits can acquire a community interest because your work on the property is community effort.

Similarly, if your broker takes care of your stock portfolio and you do nothing but an occasional "buy" or "sell," the stocks and their profits stay separate. But if you are the day-trader-in-chief, studying the market, taking advice, and doing the buys and sells–whether before work, after dinner, or throughout the day–your time is money and creates a profit to the community.

That said, pillow talk will not transmute property.

An unintentional transmutation occurred to a client of mine. She kept her inheritance from Aunt Maisie in a savings account in her own name–but deposited her paychecks into that same account. The divorce-court judge ruled that because her earnings were community property, commingling them with the separate property converted her inheritance to community. Unfair, but who can afford to appeal for a mere $35,000 sum?

Property Disposal

Whether you realize it or not, the law says you need written consent from your spouse to give away, sell, or get a lien on the things used in your home, such as "furniture, furnishings or fittings" or even your spouse's or children's "clothing or wearing apparel."

It's hard to imagine why such a law was enacted, but it is so specific, unauthorized property disposal must have once been a common or at least notorious problem. Perhaps it was written by some husband whose wife included his favorite college sweatshirt in a bundle she dropped off at Goodwill.

Another law says you cannot change the locks and kick your spouse out of your "dwelling" without a court order, even if it is your separate property.

Pre-nups

Pre-nuptial agreements provide alternatives to the "default rules" of the California Law of Rights and Obligations in Marriage noted above. If you and your spouse want to live by your own rules in marriage, write an agreement. While most pre-nups are about paychecks and money, businesses and property, you can also write in other things you care about, such as who will clean the toilet. As always, the key ingredient is valid consent.

The premarital or prenuptial agreement, or "pre-nup," you and your spouse-to-be write and sign becomes effective upon marriage. You need to follow certain procedural limits to ensure it will stand up in court, if you need it to. Most importantly, you must both fully disclose all your property and finances, including savings and debts.

The person preparing the agreement must give it to their intended spouse at least a week, seven days, before the marriage to give them time to review it with a lawyer or any other advisor.

You should both have a lawyer, but if you don't:

1. Write out the exact, specific terms and effects of the agreement

2. Write a separate document detailing what legal rights and obligations would be changed or nullified upon divorce

3. Write an express waiver of your right to a lawyer– but realize that any change to the spousal support rules will be unenforceable if the spouse entitled to support did not have a lawyer, and even if they waived their rights to one in writing.

   In fact, even if the person was represented by counsel and waived spousal support, that waiver would not be enforced if the court deems it would be "unconscionable" not to award support. If the supported person has become disabled, is unable to work, and does not have separate assets to live on, for example, the spouse who has been financially supporting them will likely be required to continue paying their support.

During Jerry Brown's first governorship, he vetoed a law that would have made premarital agreements mandatory.
He said it wasn't romantic.

Enforceable Pre-nup Clauses[2]

Your pre-nup can change the community property rules. For instance, you can make your earnings separate property and deposit your check in a separate account. Couples who agree to separate earnings usually have a third jointly owned account. They each agree to transfer a percentage of their earnings to the joint account to pay community expenses such as rent or mortgage, groceries, and entertainment. It can also:

---

2 See *Appendix 4: Marital Contract Items* for additional recommendations

- Change separate property into community property
- Waive inheritance rights
- Provide your children with more than the law requires, such as a college education
- Compensation for a spouse who contributes to the other spouse's career, such as payments for books, tuition, and sole financial support during a course of education
- Compensation to a spouse for taking time away from their own career to nurture children
- A joint parenting plan for the duration of the marriage
- A joint parenting plan in the event of separation or divorce
- Name an advocate for your children to help develop a plan in their best interests should you and your spouse be unable to agree
- A plan for how to solve problems that arise in marriage, such as mediation or couples therapy

Unenforceable Pre-nup Clauses

- Anything illegal or against "public policy," such as changing your children's legal rights to support or the court's authority to make necessary decisions "in the best interests" of a child

- Waiving rights to your spouse's employee benefit plan governed by ERISA. Only a current spouse may waive those rights, and you are not yet married.

- Changing the relationship duties of marriage, which include mutual respect, fidelity, and support.

- Eliminating the full disclosure rules in case of divorce

- Agreeing how to raise children, including indoctrination into a specific religion

I mediated a pre-nup agreement for a young couple. They wanted to assure that her parents' home did not become community property while they lived with the parents and Wife made the mortgage payments, as rent, from her earnings.

The proposed pre-nup was exchanged in a timely manner, but they each came into my office separately to sign it on their way to the church–because the groom is not supposed to see the bride before the wedding.

Post-Nups

If you did not write a pre-nup, you may still write and sign a post-nup any time during your marriage. A loving husband, for example, was concerned that his wife's impulse spending was leading to uncomfortable indebtedness. The couple went to a mediator to separate their finances and filed the agreement with their county recorder to put all creditors on official notice that their debts were no longer community, but now separate for each of them.

You and your spouse can change or revoke your pre-marital or post-marital agreements anytime provided you do it in writing, and you both sign the amendment or revocation. As with a pre-nup, write out the exact, specific terms and effects of your new agreement. Sign and date it, notarize your signatures, and record it with the county recorder's office, just to be safe and thorough.

Notionally, post-nups only allow you to change your legal relationship regarding property. However, the exceptions say you can also:

- Divide community property
- Make agreements regarding school loans or training
- Sign support agreements or separation agreements
- Agree that support will not terminate on the death of the person paying the support, and include where the money is to come from

Part 3:
Common Problems

Debts Before Marriage

Rationally, you should check your potential spouse's credit history, legal standing, and DMV record before you get married, because community property is liable for the debts either of you had before marriage. But your earnings are not, even though earnings are community property. Let's unpack that.

A creditor cannot garnish your wages for your spouse's debt for the stuff they bought back in their spendthrift days, or for the Harley that got totaled a year before you two met. But when you put your paycheck in the bank, it becomes community property, which can then be taken for your spouse's debt.

Your separate property, on the other hand, cannot be touched for the other person's pre-marital debts.

Even if you do not have a pre- or post-nup agreement, you can keep your earnings safely in a separate account in your name, and—although the account will be community property—it will not be subject to creditor attachment.

To keep your earnings as completely separate property, write a pre-nup to that effect and file it with the county recorder to give official notice.

*"When did I ever
say I was wise?
And when did I hope
that you were true?"*

Edna St. Vincent Millay
Lyrical poet and playwright

Debts During Marriage

Debts for Necessities

You are personally responsible for debts incurred by your spouse for "necessaries of life" during marriage, whether you live together or separately–unless you live separately and have a written agreement stating you are not responsible for your spouse's support.

Debts for Injuries to Another

You are liable for injury or damage your spouse caused if you were part of the actions causing the injury.

If your spouse was engaged in an activity beneficial to the community, community property pays first, before your separate property gets dinged. So if your spouse has an accident while employed as a truck driver, community property is liable. If your spouse is a doctor and injures someone in the course of surgery, the community is liable for any malpractice judgment above whatever their malpractice insurance pays.

But if your spouse was not engaged in something that benefits the community–such as having an affair, drag racing on public streets, or some other illegal activity–their separate property pays the damages, but the community is responsible if that separate property is not sufficient.

Reimbursements

If your marriage ends, you may be entitled to reimbursement for some expenses paid during marriage.

Suppose you had $10,000 in a savings account before marriage, for example, and you used all of it for a down payment on a house. The house remains community property, but you are entitled to get your $10,000 back, provided your records accurately trace its source.

You can ask for reimbursement of your share of any community property used to pay damages for your spouse's actions that were not in the community interest, including attorney fees for their criminal or civil defense.

> A profitable sideline to the divorce mill is establishing the value of property 15 or 20 years ago when a couple transmuted a house to community property in the process of refinancing. You need an expert real-estate appraiser of long experience. If you own a house when you get married, be practical and get an appraisal. Not that the worst-case scenario will come to pass–but it might have some future tax implications.

Your spouse's child or previous-marriage spousal

support is considered a debt incurred before marriage. They are obliged to use their separate funds before community funds for such support payments, and if they use community funds instead, the "community estate" is entitled to be paid back. In other words, when the community property is divided upon divorce, you can request half of whatever community money was spent on those support payments.

You must ask for reimbursement within three years of finding out about such debt payments. You must request reimbursement for injury damages within seven years, or during the dissolution of marriage proceedings. (Fam. C. §920).

In European countries, it is customary and often required to sign an agreement before marriage as to how you will treat the property you acquire, jointly or separately. These agreements can also protect property in case of bankruptcy. There is a Hague Convention on the Law Applicable to Matrimonial Property, but only five countries have signed it.

Domestic Violence

*Domestic violence is a pattern of behavior a
person uses to maintain power and control
in an intimate relationship.*

———————

*Help is available at
National Domestic Violence Hotline:
1-800-799-SAFE.*

One-third of the information provided in the
California "Your Future Together" flyer pertains to
domestic violence. The abuse plays out in a 3-phase
cycle: 1) anger, 2) abuse, 3 apologies and promises.

If you stay with an abuser, the cycle will repeat over
and over again, affecting your children, your job, your
life stability.

One out of 4 women and one out of 14 men in this
country suffer some kind of violence at the hands of a
spouse or intimate partner. Nearly 5.3 million U. S. wom-
en are victims of domestic violence each year, resulting
in 2 million injuries and 1,300 deaths.

Children in homes with violence are twice as likely to
be abused as other children.

Boys are twice as likely to become abusers as adults.

It happened in my family, generation after generation: my mother's father was jailed for beating his wife back in the 1920s. I think he broke her arm.

His son beat his wife to death. "I sat with Ruth, she was in a coma, for 11 days," my mother told me. "I burst into tears when she died. The doctor said, 'Don't cry for her, she's well out of it, away from her husband and that son of hers.'" I'll assume that son is beating his wife; I have no contact with him.

If you have children and remain in a violent relationship, social services just might take them away because you are failing to protect them.

Children

California's Uniform Parentage Act[3] adopted in 1973 established that the parent–child relationship extends equally to every child and every parent regardless of the parents' marital status. Children born to unmarried parents are equal to children born of married parents.

In other words, no one is legally born a bastard anymore. You have to choose to become one all on your own.

Both mother and father have an equal duty to support their minor children "in the manner suitable to the child's circumstances" (Fam. C. §3900). This obligation continues until the child is age 19, age 18 and finished with high school, or is self-supporting before then. There is an exception: the obligation to support a disabled child continues.

If you and your spouse agree in writing to continue support after high school, such as helping with college expenses, the court will enforce it.

During the period of support, you and your parental mate are entitled to your children's earnings—unless you're raising a child star. In that case, you could end up with just an allowance from those earnings if the court decides it's in the child's best interests.

---

3 A "Uniform" Act means that the law has been adopted by all states, such as the Uniform Premarital Agreement Act, among others.

On the other hand, your adult children are obligated to support their parents—again, to the extent of their ability—if you or your parental mate are in need and unable to maintain yourself, "except as otherwise provided by law," which is set forth in the California Welfare and Institutions Code.

If your child is incapacitated from earning a living, you and your parental mate are equally responsible to continue providing support—to the extent of your ability—when he or she becomes an adult.

Your children can be taken away if you abuse your parental authority.

They—or their aunts, uncles, cousins, or even the county—can also file a civil court request to be "freed from the dominion of the parent," and become an "emancipated minor." They would need to show the court they're already self-supporting, living away from their parents, and mature enough to run their own life.

They can become emancipated without court intervention if they marry or join any branch of the armed forces.

Your emancipated child has the privilege and right to sign contracts; approve medical care; buy, lease, and sell real property; be the plaintiff or defendant in a lawsuit; write a will; live in their own home; go to school, and get a work permit. If your child's situation changes, the court can end the emancipation and make you once again responsible for them.

Although the United States refuses to adopt the *United Nations Declaration of the Rights of the Child* (December 10, 1959,) we do recognize some of its provisions. If you do not provide a safe environment, good nutrition, healthcare, and education for your children, the state can intervene.

Your children have the constitutional right to equal protection regardless of race, gender, disability, or religion. "Special education" is an attempt to meet that constitutional right.

They are entitled to "due process," meaning notice of any sort of hearing if the state wants to take away a basic right, but their right to free speech is very limited.

They do not have a right to vote, own property, consent to medical treatment, sue or to be sued, or make binding contracts.

You can be "rendered" to another jurisdiction if you are charged with failing to support your child as described in the Uniform Interstate Family Support Act, so moving out of town, across county lines, or even to another state will not save you from child-support enforcement.

And under the Uniform Child Custody Jurisdiction and Enforcement Act, any state where your child has lived for at least 6 months has the jurisdiction to decide parenting issues.

Part 4:
Ending the Marriage

Marriage Dissolution: Divorce

Divorce, or "dissolution of marriage," typically takes at least two years in California if you engage in the default litigation process with the "assistance" of a lawyer. It can easily take five years.

You must be a California resident for 6 months and a resident of your particular county for 3 months before you can file a petition to end your marriage. And forget about charging your spouse with adultery or extreme mental cruelty. California is a "no-fault" divorce state, thanks to Governor Edmund Brown's 1966 Commission on the Family recommendations, which changed the term "divorce" to "dissolution, and "complaint" to "petition." The only reasons a court will declare a marriage dissolved are "irreconcilable differences" or "permanent legal incapacity to make decisions" (formerly insanity).

We use the same petition for marriage or domestic partnership dissolution, legal separation, annulment, or nullity.

Dissolving a Short-term Marriage

If your marriage is less than 5 years old, you can get a quick and simple "Summary Dissolution" provided:

- Both spouses sign the court form Joint Petition for Summary Dissolution

- You have no minor children and neither of you are pregnant

- Neither owns any real estate

- You have no community debts over $6,000 except car loans

- Your combined community assets are not worth more than $45,000, excluding cars

- Neither has separate property worth more than $45,000, excluding cars

- You each completed the court Income and Expense forms, following the preliminary requirements to disclose in writing:

    - Any investment, business, or income-producing

    - Any opportunities after separation based on work or investments during marriage

    - All tax returns for the past two years

- All community assets and debts and how you will divide them
- You also must mutually agree in writing to give up any right to spousal support from the other

Dissolving a Domestic Partnership

You can dissolve a domestic partnership that's less than 5 years old by filing a Notice of Termination of Domestic Partnership with the Secretary of State if you have followed all the same rules as for Summary Dissolution.

If the partnership is older than five years, you must file a petition for dissolution which is the same form as you would use for a marriage dissolution. Just check the correct box.

You can terminate a domestic partnership without the residency requirement if the state you live in does not recognize domestic partnerships.

Annulment and Nullity

Annulment is the cancellation of a marriage. Nullity decrees that no marriage ever did exist between these two people.

Annulment is not easily obtained from the court except in the case of incest (marriage between a parent and child, ancestors and descendants of every degree, siblings of half as well as whole blood, uncles or aunts and nieces or nephews) or bigamy (where one of the spouses was already married to someone else).

Otherwise, a marriage will be judged voidable if, at the time of marriage:

- The spouse asking for the annulment was under age 18

- The spouse of either party had been missing or believed dead for five years, but reappeared

- Either spouse was of "unsound mind"

- Either spouse's consent was obtained by fraud (not easy to prove)

- Either spouse's consent was obtained by force

- Either spouse was physically and incurably incapable of functioning as a married person

To persuade a judge that your consent was obtained by fraud, you must show nine particular facts:

1. That your spouse made a certain assertion or statement of a fact

2. That the fact was false

3. That the fact made a real difference in the relationship

4. That she or he knew at the time that their statement was false

5. That they intended you to take it as a true fact

6. That you had no idea the statement or fact was not true

7. That you relied on the statement or fact

8. That you acted reasonably in relying on it

9. That you suffered some damage or injury as a result of your reasonable reliance on a statement that was false.

Lies about making babies—abilities or intents—are taken more seriously than lies about addictions or wealth.

Part 5:
Appendices

A: Resources

Don't You Dare Get Married Until You Read This!
by Corey Donaldson, Three Rivers Press, $12.95.

5 Types of People Who Can Ruin Your Life:
Identifying and Dealing with Narcissists, Sociopaths, and
Other High-Conflict Personalities,
by Bill Eddy, LCSW, Esq.
(Read this early in life to help
identify personalities to avoid)

B: Declaration of the Rights of the Child[4]

1. All children have the right to what follows, no matter what their race, color sex, language, religion, political or other opinion, or where they were born or who they were born to.

2. You have the special right to grow up and to develop physically and spiritually in a healthy and normal way, free and with dignity.

3. You have a right to a name and to be a member of a country.

4. You have a right to special care and protection and to good food, housing and medical services.

5. You have the right to special care if handicapped in any way.

6. You have the right to love and understanding, preferably from parents and family, but from the government where these cannot help.

7. You have the right to go to school for free, to play, and to have an equal chance to develop yourself and to learn to be responsible and useful. Your parents have special responsibilities for your education and guidance.

---

4 Plain language version

8. You have the right always to be among the first to get help.

9. You have the right to be protected against cruel acts or exploitation, e.g. you shall not be obliged to do work which hinders your development both physically and mentally.

   a) You should not work before a minimum age and never when that would hinder your health, and your moral and physical development.

10. You should be taught peace, understanding, tolerance and friendship among all people.

C: Marital Contract Items

- Property rights, with definitions of community and how community might be converted to separate if both agree to do that

- Explanation of separate property and how separate might be converted to community property

- A plan to compensate a spouse for contributions to the career of the other, such as payments for books, tuition, and sole financial support during a course of education

- A plan to compensate a spouse for taking time away from their own career to nurture children

- A plan for joint parenting of children, including a plan in case of separation, including an advocate for children to help develop a plan in the best interests of children should the parents be unable to agree

- An acknowledgment that problems will arise between them, and that assistance to resolve problems is available through mediation to stay married or through individual and join psychotherapy

- A plan for joint parenting of any children

D: Marriage Readiness Test

Despite myths of "happily-ever-after" or "love conquers all," problems in the marital relationship may surface shortly after the wedding. The success or failure of your relationship may hinge on how well you and your spouse deal with more than just financial issues. This test is designed to help you avoid surprises about communication, conflict, parenting, in-laws, leisure time, sexuality, family of origin, spirituality, expectations, and chores.

Take some time to review it with your future spouse. You may be surprised how discussing these subjects will improve your relationship and help you avoid unrealistic expectations.

Why Are You Getting Married?

— Pregnancy

— Lust

— Obligation

— Religion

— Other _____

Finances

— Do you intend to share everything 50/50?
— Do you or your future spouse partner earn significantly more than the other or have substantially greater assets?
— How do you intend to make financial decisions?
  — Separately
  — Together
  — Spur of the moment

Money Management

— Do you intend to live within a budget?
  — Who will manage the budget?
  — Who will pay bills?
  — If you split the bills, which bill will each of you pay?
— Will you have a joint checking account?
— Will major assets be jointly held?
— What are your long-term financial goals?
  — How will you achieve them?

Daily Life

— How will you divide the household chores?
— How will you make decisions if you disagree?
— What if one partner does not fulfill their end of an agreement?
— Are you willing to work through conflict?
   — Have you been successful in the past?

Children & Parenting

— Do you want to have children? How many?
— If necessary, will you adopt?
   — Will you adopt a foreign-born child?
— How will you raise your children?
   — Will one parent stay home? If so, which parent?
— Will your children attend public or private school?
— If the marriage is not successful:
   — Who will pay child support?
   — Who will pay college expenses?

Personal Philosophy

— Do you think faith and spirituality are important in a marriage?

— Is religion an important part in your life?

— Are you comfortable discussing your sexual likes and dislikes?

— Do you mind if your spouse spends a lot of time alone or pursuing leisure activities without you?

— What will you do to make sure you have quality time together as a couple?

Part 6:
Kaluzny Marriage License Handbook Test

Marriage License Test

1. To get a marriage license, you must:
   a) Pay a fee.
   b) Change your name.
   c) Get a blood test.

2. To obtain that license you must also have:
   a) Your birth certificate.
   b) Consent of your parents.
   c) Your photo identification.

3. The person who will sign your marriage license is a:
   a) Priest.
   b) Relative.
   c) Solemnizer

4. To obtain the license you must:
   a) Apply online.
   b) Appear in person.
   c) Bring a witness.

5. After the clerk issues the license to you, you can be married
   a) In two weeks.
   b) In 24 hours.
   c) Immediately.

6. When you apply for a license, the clerk will give you:
   a) A list of health information sources.
   b) A booklet of property rights information.
   c) A booklet explaining how to obtain a divorce.

7. The most necessary part of a marriage is:
   a) A pre-nuptial agreement.
   b) Consent.
   c) Two witnesses.

8. The second necessary part of a legal marriage is:
   a) A reception.
   b) Solemnization.
   c) Kissing the bride.

9. Marriage is a:
   a) Great blessing.
   b) Church ritual.
   c) Civil contract.

10. If you are under age 18:
    a) You cannot be married.
    b) You can be married by a justice of the peace.
    c) You can marry with permission of a judge.

11. Your married name must be:
    a) The same as your spouse's.
    b) Written on your application for a license.
    c) The same as your father's.

12. A marriage license:
    a) Is good for a year.
    b) Can be renewed.
    c) Expires in 90 days.

13. The marriage license becomes your marriage certificate:
    a) When it has been filed with the county clerk.
    b) After your mother signs it.
    c) When at least one witness signs it.

14. A "confidential marriage" is:
    a) For same-sex couples only.
    b) For best friends.
    c) Not a public record.

15. Registered Domestic Partnerships are:
    a) For same-sex couples only.
    b) Not recognized by Social Security.
    c) Licensed by the county clerk.

16. Your Domestic Partner may:
   a) Adopt your child.
   b) File joint income tax returns with you.
   c) Transfer assets to you without gift or estate tax.

17. The marriage relationship is:
   a) A confidential relationship.
   b) Easy to end.
   c) Pretty cool.

18. "Confidential relationship" means:
   a) It is a secret.
   b) Your spouse is your best friend.
   c) You have a fiduciary obligation.

19. "Fiduciary" means:
   a) Best friends forever.
   b) Act with highest good faith and fair dealing.
   c) Staying faithful.

20. If you were running your own business before marriage:
   a) It is community property after marriage.
   b) It is still your separate property after marriage.
   c) Its increase in value after marriage is community.

21. If you start a business after marriage:
- a) It is community property.
- b) It is none of your spouse's business.
- c) You may run it, buying and selling as you please.

22. In managing community property:
- a) Husband is in charge of real estate.
- b) Wife is in charge of everything in the house.
- c) Wife and Husband have equal control of all community property.

23. You find out after marriage that your spouse owes a loan shark $50,000. That creditor can:
- a) Attach your wages.
- b) Just whistle for his money.
- c) Levy on your joint savings account.

24. Domestic violence:
- a) Is a crime between husband and wife.
- b) Does not hurt children.
- c) Can occur in a repeated cycle.

25. Domestic violence occurs:
- a) Very rarely.
- b) To one in four women.
- c) When the moon is full.

26. Community property includes:
   a) Your inheritance from a long-lost uncle.
   b) The stock trading account you opened in your name to celebrate your first anniversary.
   c) The gold coin you were given on your tenth birthday.

27. If your spouse tells you the cottage on the lake they inherited from their mother is now yours as a birthday gift:
   a) The cottage is now your separate property.
   b) The cottage is now community property.
   c) The cottage is still belongs to your spouse.

28. The house you owned before marriage remains entirely separate property if:
   a) It has no mortgage.
   b) You pay the mortgage with direct deposit from your salary.
   c) Your spouse says it is okay to use the joint bank account.

29. If you leave your spouse who is unemployed:
   a) They had better go out and get a job.
   b) You still owe a duty to support your spouse.
   c) They can go live with their parents.

30. Charges on credit cards in your spouse's name only:
   a)   Are their separate debt.
   b)   Can be paid from your joint checking account.
   c)   Are against the fiduciary obligation.

31. Your spouse breaks someone's arm in a barroom fight, and he is sued:
   a)   You should file for bankruptcy.
   b)   The spouse must pay damages from his income.
   c)   The community is not responsible unless the spouse has no separate property.

32. You can get an annulment of your marriage if:
   a)   You were married only one year.
   b)   You didn't sleep with your spouse.
   c)   Your spouse is incurably impotent.

33. That legacy from your grandmother becomes community property if:
   a)   You buy stocks in your own name with the money.
   b)   You deposit it into the bank account with your spouse.
   c)   You tell your spouse you will share it.

34. No child born in California:
   a)   Can have a job.
   b)   Is illegitimate.
   c)   Has to support a parent.

35. A child over age 18 must be supported:
   a)   If a girl, until she is married.
   b)   If he doesn't have a job.
   c)   If they haven't finished high school.

36. If a couple purchases a house as "tenants in common":
   a)   Either one can sell his or her half.
   b)   In case one dies, the other becomes sole owner.
   c)   The children own shares in the property.

37. A premarital agreement is not enforceable if:
   a)   Your fiancé didn't have a lawyer.
   b)   You agree to support any children by yourself.
   c)   You do not have any separate property.

38. A premarital agreement must:
   a)   Be given to the other party not less than seven days before the wedding.
   b)   Be reviewed by lawyers for both husband and wife.
   c)   State that your wages are your separate property.

39. An incapacitated child must be:
  a) Placed in an institution.
  b) Supported by parents after age 18.
  c) Supported by the State.

40. A business you start after marriage is separate property if:
  a) You can keep it a secret from your spouse.
  b) It is in your name only.
  c) Your spouse signs an agreement that it is yours alone.

True or False

1. ___T ___F   If you did not sign a premarital agreement, you must abide by California community property law during your entire marriage.

2. ___T ___F   You and spouse have a big fight. You owned the house before you married, so you can change the locks to keep that mean person out.

3. ___T ___F   There are no witnesses to a confidential marriage

4. ___T ___F   A marriage certificate is a public record.

5. ___T ___F   Any two people can have a valid domestic partnership by registering the correct paperwork with the state.

6. ___T ___F   Half the husband's pension can be given to wife, but a pension she earns is hers.

7. ___T ___F A savings account in wife's name is her separate property.

8. ___T ___F Real property purchased in Husband's name when he is married is his separate property.

9. ___T ___F Once you separate, anything you can avoid telling your spouse about is yours.

10. ___T ___F Domestic violence is grounds for divorce.

Test Answers

1. a)
2. c)
3. c)
4. a) COVID
   protocols
5. c)
6. a)
7. b)
8. b)
9. c)
10. c)
11. b)
12. c)
13. a)
14. c)
15. b)
16. a)
17. a)
18. c)
19. b)
20. b)
21. a)
22. c)

23. c)
24. c)
25. b)
26. b)
27. c)
28. a)
29. b)
30. b)
31. c)
32. c)
33. b)
34. b)
35. c)
36. a)
37. b)
38. a)
39. b)
40. c)

True-false questions
1. T
2. F

3. T
4. T
5. T
6. F
7. F
8. F
9. F
10. F

www.ingramcontent.com/pod-product-compliance
Lightning Source LLC
Chambersburg PA
CBHW060339130626
46553CB00003B/1058